Core 1 (220-1101) Exam Topics

Mobile Devices

Laptop Hardware and Components:

Understanding the internal and external components of laptops is crucial.

This includes the installation and configuration of various hardware components like keyboards, touchpads, and different types of displays.

You should be able to identify and replace components such as hard drives, RAM, and battery packs.

Familiarity with types of displays like LCD, LED, and OLED, and knowing how to replace them, is also important.

2024 Comprehensive Guide to the CompTIA A+ Certification

The CompTIA A+ certification is an essential stepping stone for IT professionals, providing foundational knowledge and skills in a wide range of IT domains.

This certification is globally recognized and often considered a prerequisite for many IT roles. Whether you're starting your career or seeking to validate your skills, the CompTIA A+ certification is a critical credential to have.

Overview of the CompTIA A+ Certification

The CompTIA A+ certification comprises two separate exams:
1. Core 1 (220-1101)
2. Core 2 (220-1102)

Each exam covers different aspects of IT, including hardware, networking, mobile devices, operating systems, security, and troubleshooting. Together, these exams ensure that candidates possess the knowledge necessary to perform essential IT support and operational roles.

Mobile Device Network Connectivity:

Mobile devices often require different methods for connecting to networks compared to traditional desktops or laptops.

You must understand how to configure and troubleshoot wireless networks, Bluetooth connections, and mobile hotspots. Knowledge of cellular technologies like GSM, CDMA, LTE, and 5G is essential.

Mobile Device Synchronization:

Synchronization involves the process of ensuring data is consistent across different devices.

You need to be familiar with various synchronization methods, including cloud synchronization, synchronization to a desktop or laptop, and syncing with email servers. Understanding how to sync contacts, email, and other data types between devices and services is critical.

Networking

Networking Concepts:

Basic networking concepts form the backbone of IT knowledge.

You should be well-versed in IP addressing (IPv4 and IPv6), understanding subnetting, and the function of DNS and DHCP in network communications.

Knowledge of network topologies (e.g., star, mesh, bus) and protocols (e.g., TCP/IP, UDP) is also essential.

Network Hardware:

Identifying and using network hardware is a core skill.

This includes knowledge of different types of network cables (e.g., CAT5, CAT6, fiber optic), connectors (e.g., RJ-45, coaxial), and tools (e.g., crimping tools, cable testers).

You should understand how to set up and configure routers, switches, and access points.

Wireless Networking:

Wireless networking involves understanding standards such as IEEE 802.11 (Wi-Fi standards), the differences between them (e.g., 802.11a, b, g, n, ac, ax), and the implications for speed and range.

Knowledge of wireless security protocols (e.g., WEP, WPA, WPA2, WPA3) is crucial for securing wireless networks.

Hardware

Motherboards, CPUs, and Power Supplies:

You must be able to identify various types of motherboards (e.g., ATX, Micro-ATX), CPUs (e.g., Intel, AMD), and power supplies.

Installation, configuration, and troubleshooting of these components are key skills. Understanding the function of BIOS/UEFI and how to update firmware is also important.

RAM and Storage:

Different types of RAM (e.g., DDR3, DDR4) and storage devices (e.g., HDDs, SSDs, NVMe) are covered.

You should know how to install and configure these devices, and understand the impact of different storage technologies on performance.

Peripheral Devices:

Installation and configuration of peripheral devices such as printers, scanners, and external storage devices are also covered.

Knowledge of various printer types (e.g., laser, inkjet, thermal) and their maintenance is essential.

Virtualization and Cloud Computing

Virtualization:

Virtualization is the creation of a virtual version of something, such as a hardware platform, operating system, or storage device.

You should understand the basics of virtualization, the role of hypervisors (e.g., Type 1 and Type 2), and how virtual machines (VMs) operate.

Cloud Computing:

Cloud computing involves delivering different services over the internet.

Understanding cloud models (IaaS, PaaS, SaaS), deployment models (public, private, hybrid), and the benefits of cloud services (e.g., scalability, cost-efficiency) is crucial.

Hardware and Network Troubleshooting

Troubleshooting Methodology:

Effective troubleshooting involves following a structured methodology: identifying the problem, establishing a theory of probable cause, testing the theory, establishing a plan of action, implementing the solution, and verifying full system functionality.

Common Hardware Problems:

Identification and resolution of common hardware issues such as no power, overheating, and display problems are essential.

You should know how to diagnose issues with RAM, hard drives, and peripheral devices.

Common Network Problems:

Network troubleshooting skills include identifying and resolving connectivity issues, IP conflicts, slow network performance, and wireless signal problems.

Familiarity with network diagnostic tools (e.g., ping, traceroute, ipconfig) is important.

Core 2 (220-1102) Exam Topics

Operating Systems

Windows OS Installation and Configuration:

Windows OS is widely used in businesses and homes. You should understand the installation process, configuration settings, and how to manage user accounts and permissions.

Knowledge of Windows features like Group Policy, Active Directory, and remote desktop is also important.

Other Operating Systems:

While Windows is prominent, you should also have basic knowledge of macOS, Linux, and mobile operating systems (iOS, Android).

This includes installation, basic configuration, and common commands used for troubleshooting.

Command Line Tools:

Command line tools are powerful for troubleshooting and configuration.

You should be familiar with commands for file management (e.g., dir, ls), network diagnostics (e.g., ping, traceroute), and system configuration (e.g., ipconfig, netstat).

Security

Security Fundamentals:

Understanding basic security concepts, such as types of threats (e.g., malware, phishing), vulnerabilities, and risk management, is essential.

Knowledge of authentication methods (e.g., passwords, biometrics) and the principles of confidentiality, integrity, and availability (CIA triad) is crucial.

Security Best Practices:

Implementing security best practices involves using strong passwords, enabling firewalls, updating software regularly, and educating users about social engineering attacks.

Knowledge of encryption methods and security policies is also important.

Workstation Security:

 Configuring workstation security settings includes setting up antivirus software, managing user permissions, and using security tools like BitLocker for disk encryption.

 You should understand the importance of physical security measures as well.

Software Troubleshooting

Troubleshooting Methodology:

Software troubleshooting follows a similar methodology to hardware troubleshooting.

Identifying the problem, establishing a theory, testing the theory, implementing a solution, and verifying the result are key steps.

Windows OS Troubleshooting:

Common Windows issues include blue screen errors, slow performance, and application crashes.

You should know how to use tools like Task Manager, Event Viewer, and System Restore to diagnose and resolve issues.

Application Troubleshooting:

Troubleshooting application issues involves checking compatibility, reinstalling software, and verifying configurations.

Understanding how to resolve issues with web browsers, office applications, and other common software is important.

Operational Procedures

Best Practices:

Following best practices for safety involves using proper tools and techniques to prevent injuries and equipment damage.

Environmental practices include proper disposal of electronic waste and adherence to regulatory standards.

Documentation and Professionalism:

Maintaining detailed documentation of configurations, changes, and issues is crucial for troubleshooting and compliance.

Professionalism involves clear communication, ethical behavior, and continuous learning to stay updated with technological advancements.

Study Tips and Resources

Use Official Study Materials

Utilize the official CompTIA A+ study guides and resources.

These materials are designed to cover all exam objectives and provide practice questions and scenarios that mimic the actual exams.

Hands-On Practice

Set up a home lab to gain practical experience. Build and disassemble computers, configure networks, install different operating systems, and practice troubleshooting common issues.

Real-world experience is invaluable for understanding the concepts and procedures covered in the exams.

Practice Exams

Taking practice exams helps you familiarize yourself with the format and types of questions you'll encounter.

Identify areas where you need improvement and focus your studies on those topics.

Online Resources

There are numerous online resources available, including video tutorials, forums, and interactive labs.

Websites like CompTIA's official site, Professor Messer, and various IT forums provide valuable study materials and community support.

Join Study Groups

Joining study groups or online communities allows you to discuss topics, share resources, and get help with difficult concepts.

Engaging with others can provide new insights and make studying more interactive and enjoyable.

Conclusion

The CompTIA A+ certification is a fundamental credential for aspiring IT professionals.

It covers a wide range of topics, ensuring candidates have a comprehensive understanding of IT systems and troubleshooting techniques.

By studying the key areas outlined in the Core 1 and Core 2 exams, utilizing various study resources, and gaining hands-on experience, you can effectively prepare for and pass the certification exams.

Achieving the CompTIA A+ certification not only validates your skills but also opens doors to numerous career opportunities in the IT field.

It serves as a strong foundation for further certifications and career advancement, making it a valuable investment in your professional development.

Please use the next few pages for your notes.